# The Dust Bowl

# THE DUST BOWL

## DISASTER ON THE PLAINS

**TRICIA ANDRYSZEWSKI**

*Spotlight on American History*
*The Millbrook Press • Brookfield, Connecticut*

Excerpts from *Dust Bowl Diary,* by Ann Marie Low,
by permission of University of Nebraska Press.
Copyright 1984 by the University of Nebraska Press.

Cover photograph courtesy of
Dallas Museum of Art, Dallas Art Association Purchase
Map by Joe LeMonnier
Photos courtesy of: the Library of Congress: pp. 9, 14–15, 18,
23, 24, 27, 32, 35, 37, 38–39, 41, 44, 50; Kansas State Historical
Society: p. 21 (both); UPI/Bettmann: p. 29; Soil Conservation
Service, USDA: pp. 47, 49, 52, 57.

Library of Congress Cataloging-in-Publication Data
Andryszewski, Tricia, 1956–
The Dust Bowl/Disaster on the Plains / by Tricia Andryszewski.
p.   cm.—(Spotlight on American history)
Includes bibliographical references and index.
Summary: Examines the human and natural causes of the severe dust
storms that turned much of the Great Plains into a "dust bowl" in
the 1930s and describes the devastation caused by these storms.
ISBN 1-56294-272-7 (lib. bdg.)
1. Dust storms—Great Plains—History—20th century—Juvenile
literature.   2. Great Plains—Social conditions—Juvenile literature.
3. Depressions—1929—Great Plains—Juvenile literature.   4. Agriculture—Great Plains—History—20th century—Juvenile literature.
5. Droughts—Great Plains—History—20th century—Juvenile literature.   [1. Dust storms—Great Plains.   2. Droughts—Great Plains—
History.   3. Agriculture—Great Plains—History.   4. Depressions—
1929.   5. Great Plains—History.]   I. Title.   II. Series.
F595.A57   1993        978—dc20        92-15300   CIP   AC

Published by The Millbrook Press
2 Old New Milford Road
Brookfield, Connecticut 06804

# Contents

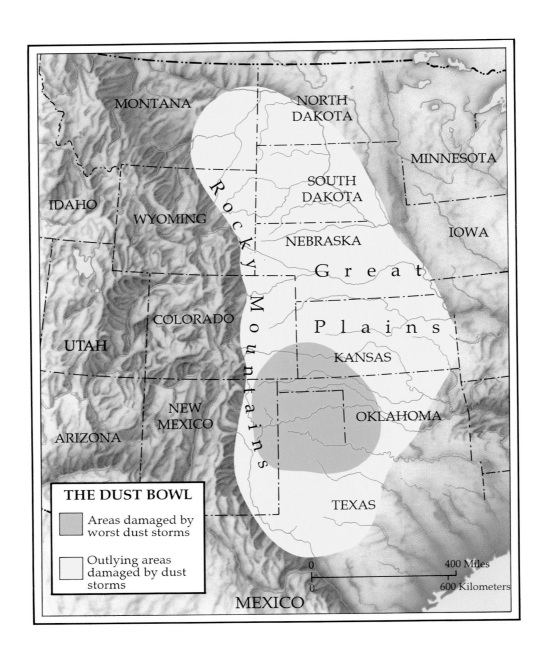

THE DUST BOWL

Areas damaged by worst dust storms

Outlying areas damaged by dust storms

# *Introduction*

*The mess was incredible! Dirt had blown into the house all week and lay inches deep on everything. Every towel and curtain was just black. There wasn't a clean dish or cooking utensil. . . . Life in what the newspapers call "the Dust Bowl" is becoming a gritty nightmare.*

THE DUST BOWL. Today we think of dust storms the way we think of tornadoes, hurricanes, and earthquakes: natural disasters that begin and end suddenly, leaving behind terrible damage. But, for people living on the Great Plains in the 1930s, the dust storms came again and again, leaving no chance for people to recover. In many places and for much of the year the sky was filled with dust on more days than it was clear. Dust storms became a way of life on the Great Plains, and especially in the area that came to be called the Dust Bowl.

Just where was this Dust Bowl, with its terrible black blizzards? A tourist in the 1930s asked a Kansas wheat farmer this question, and the farmer answered: "Stay where you are, and it'll come to you." The boundaries of the Dust Bowl shifted from year to year, and from storm to storm. Dust storms devastated farmland from Texas all the way to North Dakota. The area hardest and most consistently hit—50 million acres (20 million hectares) in Oklahoma, Texas, New Mexico, Colorado, and Kansas—was what most people called the Dust Bowl.

The dust storms began in 1932, and the first big one came in November 1933. It covered a huge area: from Montana east to the Great Lakes and south to the lower Mississippi River valley. But it wasn't until the spring of 1934 that the whole nation woke up to this enormous problem.

In early May 1934, a big storm—bigger than any other that anyone could remember—blew for thirty-six hours. Its dust cloud covered 1,500 miles (2,400 kilometers) from the Rocky Mountains east to the Great Lakes by 900 miles (1,450 kilometers) from Canada south to Oklahoma. This storm and many others picked up millions of tons of soil from the Great Plains and carried it on the wind over the eastern half of the country, dropping much of it over Chicago, Pittsburgh—even New York, Washington, and other eastern cities. Dust from the Great Plains even fell on ships as far as 500 miles (800 kilometers) out to sea in the Atlantic Ocean.

It's hard to believe, but 1935 was even worse than 1934. On Black Sunday—April 14, 1935—a terrible black blizzard swept over the Great Plains, blotting out the sun and causing outdoor temperatures to drop by as much as fifty degrees in only a few hours. During the summer of that year, the ceilings of some homes collapsed from the weight of all the dust that had accumulated in attics!

*A dust storm sweeps across the plains in the 1930s at the height of the Dust Bowl era.*

Eventually, the tide turned, and life slowly returned to normal. But this took years of work and cooperation from people and from nature. And, in some ways, life on the Great Plains was never the same again. For, although dust storms are a natural phenomenon, human activities played a large role in creating the Dust Bowl, and those activities had to change.

What caused the Dust Bowl? Why did the black blizzards finally end? Why haven't they returned? Can it ever happen again?

# 1

## NATURE'S ROLE

*A perfect cloud of dust and sand filled the air and dusted in every crack and crevice of the buildings, and the unlucky pedestrian who was compelled to be abroad absorbed the full peck of dirt that is allotted to each one's life, and what his or her stomach would not hold was stowed away in their ears, eyes and clothing. The flies laid low; the dogs crawled into the cellars, and the birds nestled closely wherever shelter could be found.*

ANOTHER 1930s Dust Bowl story? Not quite. This description of a dust storm was printed in a Kansas newspaper—in 1883. Dust storms, it seems, happened occasionally on the Great Plains long before the name "Dust Bowl" was invented. In fact, they are an inevitable part of the ecology of the region.

Before any people lived there, the Great Plains was a vast sea of grass covering a flat (or in some places rolling) landscape that had few trees and little water. This was a very different kind of ecosystem, or environment, from that found in the Rocky Mountains to the west and in the naturally forested lands east of the Mississippi.

Mixed-grasses and short-grasses are the natural prairie vegetation of the region so badly damaged by dust storms in the 1930s. Mixed-grass prairie is covered mostly by grasses that naturally grow 2 to 4 feet (0.6 to 1.2 meters) high; the grasses of short-grass prairie are less than 2 feet (0.6 meters) tall. These two kinds of prairie vegetation are not separated by sharp boundaries—they blur into each other, and the transition zone between the two shifts over time. Short-grass prairie needs less rainfall than mixed-grass prairie. In years of plentiful rain, mixed-grass prairie will move into areas that are usually covered by short-grass prairie. In other years, during a drought (a period of extreme dryness), the shorter grasses will take over some areas that are usually mixed-grass prairie.

Why did so few trees grow on the prairie? The simplest answer is the lack of water: There's just not enough rainfall for most trees. About 20 inches (50 centimeters) of rain usually fall each year in the mixed-grass prairie region. Rainfall decreases as you head west. The drier parts of the short-grass prairie area average as little as 10 inches (25 centimeters) of rain each year.

Worse, what little rain there is falls mostly in the spring, with another rainy season sometimes coming in the fall. For the rest of the year, there is drought.

Worse still, rainfall varies a lot from year to year. Sometimes ten years or more of good rainfall will be followed by years of drought, when as little as half the normal amount of rain might fall. Not many trees can cope with months of drought each year, especially when whole years—sometimes more—of even worse drought occur from time to time.

Wind makes the lack of rain even harder for prairie plants to handle. Wind blows steadily across the prairie, encouraging evaporation of whatever water it crosses. Evaporation takes water from where it can be used by prairie plants and animals. Evaporation is especially severe during the hot summers in the southern parts of the region, and in the short-grass areas, where winds blow harder.

The constant wind also contributes to another natural prairie phenomenon: fire. Prairie grass provides an ideal fuel for fires started by lightning or by people. Wind fans the fire and pushes it along, and there are few rivers in the region to stop it.

If the lack of water weren't enough to keep trees from growing, the regular fires would be. Fires kill trees, but grasses are well suited to survive them. Grasses often grow even better after a fire, which clears away years of dead stalks, allowing light and air to reach new growth at ground level.

Although the prairie seems like a very harsh environment, many animals have found a home there, and some could not live anywhere else. The largest and most famous of these animals is the American bison. A single bison bull can weigh over a ton and stand 7 feet (2 meters) tall. In the 1800s, millions of these huge animals roamed the mixed-grass prairie, often in herds of tens of thousands. The herds moved constantly, grazing one area until little grass was left, then moving on.

The bison played an important role in the prairie ecosystem. If the rains cooperated, the grass grazed by bison—like a sheared lawn—grew back lush and green. Prairie dogs (chipmunk-like rodents that form large packs and live in underground burrows) often moved into an area grazed by bison. With the grass cut short, the prairie dogs could see danger—a coyote or a snake, for example—a long way off, giving them time to reach the safety of the burrow.

Bison roamed the dry, almost treeless prairie searching for what little vegetation they could find. As soon as one area was grazed clean, the bison would move on, leaving behind vast stretches of dusty soil.

Prairie dogs, in turn, helped the bison—although not intentionally. Bison enjoyed wallowing in dirt, probably because it helped to rid them of insects and mats of their thick fur. They often visited prairie dog "towns" to dig up the burrows and wallow in the loose dirt—a task much easier than digging up tough prairie sod. Bison-wallowing sometimes created deep hollows that collected rainwater and became watering holes for prairie animals.

The prairie grasses and the bison, prairie dogs, and other animals were well adapted to their environment. But even these tough natives had a hard time of it in years of drought. Without rain, grass stops growing. Without fresh growth to eat, prairie animals graze the grass down to the ground, then paw at the stubble or even dig up the roots, looking for more food. This activity, combined with prairie fires and the stress of the drought, kills some patches of grass and thins out much of the rest of it.

Without the roots of the grass to hold it in place, the fine prairie soil drifts like sand dunes. A good, strong wind—common on the prairie—will pick this dusty soil up and carry it for miles. If dry weather lasts for several years, many dust storms will blow across the prairie.

But even during the worst of droughts in a natural prairie ecosystem the dust storms would never make a Dust Bowl. That could happen only after decades of human activities altered the fragile prairie ecosystem, making it much more vulnerable to the harshest effects of a long drought.

# 2

## THE HUMAN CONTRIBUTION

THE FIRST PEOPLE to live on the Great Plains were the Plains Indians. For thousands of years they lived in harmony with the fragile prairie. Most of their food came from hunting and from the gardens of maize (corn) and vegetables carefully cultivated in the region's riverbeds and streambeds. They hunted the prairie bison, pronghorn, jackrabbits, and other animals, using the meat for food, the skins for warmth, and even the skeletons for tools.

This way of life began to change when the Plains Indians acquired horses, which were first brought to the Americas by Spanish explorers and colonizers. On horseback, the Indians could hunt the bison much more effectively. By early in the 1700s, many Plains Indians had become completely dependent on the bison for food, clothing, and even shelter.

Although the Plains Indians killed bison in great numbers, the total number of bison on the prairie might well have grown during this period. As late as 1870, between 30 and 70 million bison roamed the prairie. But only thirty years later, fewer than one thousand

*A passenger train steams across the plains near Custer City, North Dakota. The introduction of the railroad to the Great Plains in the late 1800s strained the land in many ways.*

bison were left. This amazing drop in the bison population was caused not by Indian hunting, but by the arrival—for the first time— of large numbers of English-speaking settlers.

Beginning in the mid-1800s, more and more settlers were lured to the prairie from the eastern part of the United States. The Homestead Act of 1862 granted farmers free western land if they would agree to live on it and farm it for at least five years. Another development in the 1800s was the railroads that were built across the prairie. Now ranch and farm produce could be shipped back to markets in the East. It became possible for more and more people to "make a living" on the Great Plains.

Sadly, the U.S. government decided to force the Plains Indians onto reservations to make way for the new settlers. The government also encouraged the killing of millions of buffalo, so that domesticated cattle and sheep could replace them on the vast grazing lands of the Great Plains.

Most of the early settlers were ranchers, but, by the 1880s, many farmers had begun to move into the area. A drought in the 1890s sent some of these farmers back where they came from, but the turn of the century brought years of better rainfall—and still more farmers—to the prairie.

Wheat was the crop that most of these farmers wanted to grow, and they plowed up millions of acres—32 million acres (12 million hectares) just between 1909 and 1932—of tough prairie sod to plant it. The sod they removed was so tough, and trees in the region so scarce, that early farmers used blocks of sod instead of timber to build houses.

At the time, all of this plowing seemed like a good idea. Underneath the tough layer of sod was some of the richest topsoil in the country. Wheat grew well in this soil—when the rains came.

[ 19 ]

And from the 1890s through the 1920s there was usually enough rain. With the help of more and better farming equipment introduced over these years, a farmer could work more and more acres, earning more money with less labor. True, the farmers had to pay for their new plows and other equipment, but wheat brought a good enough price at the market even in the early years of this period. Then, when World War I came to Europe in 1914 and farm production there decreased, the demand for American wheat increased. The price farmers were paid for wheat doubled! This long period of decent rain and good prices led many farmers to believe they had found "wheat heaven."

Trouble for the farmers began when the war ended, on November 11, 1918. Thanks to the farmers' hard work, they were now producing more wheat than the world had ever seen. But Europe no longer needed it, now that its own farmers were back at work. In 1920 prices dropped, and they stayed low. Farmers had to break more and more sod to plant more wheat just to make the same amount of money. Worse still, the farmers still owed money on their tractors and other improved farming equipment and many farmers had mortgages to pay to banks. Many others didn't even own the land they farmed and had to pay rent to landlords. All of these bills had to be paid, and the amount due didn't drop when wheat prices did.

Trouble for the land began even earlier. Farmers and ranchers used up the land's resources faster than nature could renew them. As more and more land was plowed up and planted with wheat, the amount of land available for grassy pasture shrank—but the number of cattle and sheep didn't. More and more animals on less land led to overgrazing—having more animals on the prairie than it could continue to support.

*Top:* A family poses in front of their house, built of sod blocks and dug into the prairie. Even the roof is covered with sod.
*Bottom:* The early 1900s were boom years for growing wheat on the Great Plains. Prices were high and rain was plentiful.

Other farming practices were poor as well. For example, instead of plowing under the plant stubble left on the fields after crops were harvested, farmers usually burned it off or allowed livestock to graze it to the ground. Plowing under crop residues adds organic material to the soil. Organic matter gives good soil its rich, chocolate-cake texture and helps hold it together. With less and less of this organic matter left, plowing and cultivation pulverized the soil more and more.

An especially dangerous effect of the various poor farming practices was that precious water—never too plentiful on the Great Plains—was wasted. In a natural prairie ecosystem, water in years of good rainfall percolates down through the topsoil to the subsoil, where it collects in a reservoir of moisture that is tapped by the prairie plants in dry years. But with the soil stripped of its protective covering of sod, overcultivated, and overgrazed, water was lost to evaporation or used up as soon as rain fell. During the years of good rainfall lasting through the 1920s, the prairie's natural reservoir was emptied—not refilled, as it should have been. There would be no water there when it was needed.

And it certainly was needed in the 1930s. The years of good rain gave way to the worst drought on record, beginning in 1931 and lasting through 1937. During those years, twenty states set records for dryness that have not been matched since. Rainfall was as little as half the normal amount. During most of these years there was not even enough winter snow to keep the ground covered and prevent evaporation of what little water was left in the soil. And it was hot as well as dry: Summertime highs reached 100 to 120 degrees Fahrenheit (38 to 49 degrees Celsius) in many places.

Farmers still tried to grow wheat. But cultivating the prairie soil—already in poor condition in many places—in dry years caused

*The drought of the 1930s turned what were once prosperous farms into dust-covered wastelands.*

it to break down into a fine dust. As the drought wore on, the little rain that fell did less and less good, because soil that has turned to dust can't easily absorb water—it just rolls right off. Wheat grew poorly or not at all under these conditions. With no wheat roots to hold the ground in place, there was nothing to prevent wind erosion. The soil that had turned to dust blew away on the wind. The dust storms began.

The prairie wind picked up this fine dust and blew it in drifts, smothering what few living plants were left. As the dust blew, it broke apart into even smaller particles. The finer the dust became, the less wind was needed to pick it up and blow it around. And so the dust storms became worse and more frequent as the drought went on. The dust became so fine, so lightweight, that once it was in the air it tended to hang there, settling only very slowly to earth. So, even when there *weren't* dust storms, it was always dusty across much of what had been the prairie. This was the Dust Bowl.

# The Grapes of Wrath

*A day went by and the wind increased, steady, unbroken by gusts. The dust from the roads fluffed up and spread out and fell on the weeds beside the fields, and fell into the fields a little way. . . . The wind grew stronger. . . . The finest dust did not settle back to earth now, but disappeared into the darkening sky.*

This convincing description of the beginning of a dust storm wasn't written by an eyewitness. Instead, it comes at the beginning of a novel—John Steinbeck's *The Grapes of Wrath*.

Steinbeck's novel and the movie it inspired tell most of what people today know about the Dust Bowl. The book's fictional family, the Joads, were forced off their small Oklahoma farm when the bank that owned it decided to replace their labor with that of a tractor. Like thousands of real-life "Okies," defeated by dust and poverty, the Joads drove across the Dust Bowl to California, where they dreamed of beginning a new and better life. But jobs were scarce, and they became migrant farmworkers under harsher conditions than what they had left behind in the Dust Bowl.

Steinbeck, who lived in California, didn't get all of the details of the Dust Bowl exactly right. The Joads planted cotton, not wheat like most Dust Bowl farmers. And the part of Oklahoma where the Joads lived wasn't even very hard hit by the Dust Bowl. But Steinbeck's book did unforgettably capture the heartbreaking story of the Okies and the flavor of that terrible time and place. His bestselling novel has become an American classic.

*Facing page: A migrant worker and her children, 1936, by famed photographer Dorothea Lange.*

# 3

## LIFE IN THE DUST BOWL

**NOVEMBER 9, 1929, SATURDAY:**
*There seems to be quite a furor in the country over a big stock market crash that wiped a lot of people out. We are ahead of them. The hailstorm in July of 1928 and bank failure that fall wiped out a lot of people locally. As far as that goes, North Dakota was hard hit last year.*

*Due to low prices Dad has decided to keep his cattle over winter. A lot of people have to sell for lack of feed. Dad and Bud and I put up plenty of hay. Maybe next year we won't have to work so hard. There may be plenty of rain and hay. Cattle prices may go up.*

DUST AND DROUGHT weren't the only problems Great Plains farmers faced in the 1930s—there was also the Great Depression. Beginning with the stock market crash in 1929, the entire American economy collapsed. Banks closed. Millions of people saw their life savings disappear and were left with no money. Many lost their homes. Millions of people were out of work, more of the popula-

*During the Depression, businessmen used to high-paying jobs
were seen on the streets selling apples to support their families.*

tion than has ever been unemployed since. And those who still had jobs made much less money than they used to. Farm families, too, got less money at the market for the farm goods they sold.

Ann Marie Low, her brother Bud, and her parents lived on a farm in North Dakota. Ann kept a diary during the Dust Bowl years. She was only seventeen years old when she wrote the paragraphs at the beginning of this chapter, but she was already working hard on her family's farm. The description of their house after a dust storm quoted at the beginning of this book comes from Ann's diary. Other diary entries appear below. Through her diary, Ann tells us what it was like to live in the Dust Bowl.

Even during the best of years, the margin between success and failure for farmers in the worst-hit part of the Dust Bowl was slim. Only the best farmers could get by. Conditions were, and still are, better for farming where the Lows lived. Many farmers had it worse than the Low family did during the Dust Bowl years, but even the Lows found the 1930s terrible. In 1929, Ann hoped that better times were ahead. She didn't know that the drought and hard times were only beginning:

*Dad says the sheriff has an order from a bank to kick Grover Stern off his farm. . . . Thank goodness, Dad hates mortgages and won't mortgage this place come hell or high water. These mortgaged farms! Old Man Ziets was living on one. He got a crop of one bushel to the acre. While he was harvesting last fall, the bankers owning the mortgage drove out in the field and bawled him out for not having a better crop.*

*Ziets stepped off the binder. "Chentlemen, here you are. Chust help yourselfs." He walked off the field and off the farm.*

*A man who had the mortgage on them came and took the horses. Another mortgagee took the machinery. The bankers had a hard time getting the grain harvested.*

*Ziets hopped a freight train to Montana, where he is mining or lumbering or something.*

Unlike Ziets—and unlike the "Okies" portrayed in *The Grapes of Wrath*—most farmers stayed on their farms. It helped that most family farms, like the Lows's farm, grew a variety of crops. Farmers who grew only wheat were in the worst trouble: Wheat wouldn't grow in the drought, and the price they got for what little they could grow was about one quarter of what they had gotten during the good years of the late 1920s. The Lows grew some wheat, but they also raised cattle, grew hay and other feed for the cattle, raised chickens and turkeys, grew flax for the market, and kept a garden for their own kitchen. All of these crops were hurt by the drought, but some were hurt more than others. Growing a variety of foods gave them a better chance to get by.

**JUNE 1, 1930, SUNDAY:**
*Yesterday Bud and I cultivated corn. The wind blew the whole oat field on us. . . .*

*The wind and dirt are really moving. There is so much dirt in the air, even in the barn, one can't see clearly. A white setting hen in the barn is so dirty not a white feather shows. Dad's oats have already blown out, and the flax may go, too. My baby chickens are blowing to death. I've had to lock them in the calf shed for shelter.*

*Ted Roy told about the trouble he is having with his crop. He put it in and it blew out. He seeded again and it blew out. So he went fishing. His little daughter piped up, "And Mama cried."*

**JUNE 18, 1930, WEDNESDAY:**
*The flax is nearly gone now—blown out. It is too bad. We really need the money that flax would have brought.*

[ 31 ]

*Many families fled the Dust Bowl, hoping to find work
in other parts of the country. In this 1936 photo, a farmer's
wife and children wait patiently while he fixes a tire during
their journey from southern Texas to Arkansas.*

*Mama . . . has always hated the wind and tells that in California when she was young she could put her hat on at a certain angle and it would stay that way all day. Dad says when he came here there was nothing to stop the wind between here and the North Pole. He broke its power some by putting up a barbed wire fence. He can always make Mama laugh.*

Laughter was precious during these hard times, and people told jokes and tall stories about the heat, the wind, and the dust. One story had it that a man hit on the head by a raindrop was so overcome by this strange experience that a bucketful of dust had to be poured over his head to revive him.

Another tall story was set after a whopper of a dust storm. A traveler noticed a nice new hat by the side of the road, and he stopped to pick it up. Under the hat was a man, buried up to his neck in the dust! As he dug the poor fellow out, the traveler asked if he wanted a ride into town. "No, I'll get there myself," the man replied, "I'm on a horse."

**JULY 26, 1931, SUNDAY:**
*Yesterday was so hot the men didn't go in the fields in the afternoon for fear of killing the horses. The thermometer registered 114 degrees. Dad didn't believe it, so he put out another thermometer. It registered 116 degrees. I picked and canned peas most of the day.*

**AUGUST 1, 1931, SATURDAY:**
*Thursday we rounded up the cattle to ship. It was raining that day, but too late to do the feed situation any good. In the morning we took all but the best breeding stock from the Big Pasture, then went south to get most of the yearlings.*

*It is a shame. Dad has been building up this herd for years and now is having to sell a lot of stock he depended on to carry on the herd. It will take years to build it up again. He won't get any price now. The bottom has dropped clear out of the market. There is just no feed in the country, and cattle are being shipped by the thousands.*

The drought was hard on livestock. Without rain, the hay and grains cattle eat won't grow. Without enough feed to go around, farmers had to sell their cattle—whether they were large enough to market or not—or see them starve. Millions of cattle were brought to the market, far more than there were buyers for in the depressed economy. Prices dropped to a fraction of what they had been during the good years before the drought.

**MARCH 7, 1933, TUESDAY:**
*Dad was driving the teams [of horses] to town with a load of wheat to sell in order to buy coal. President Roosevelt has declared a bank holiday. Dad couldn't sell the wheat and had to bring it back. He was really upset when he came into the house to break the sad news that evening.*

*I said, "Money is only a symbol, anyway."*

*He glared at me.*

*Mama, who was playing gin rummy with Bud, said, "Never mind, Dearie, you still have me."*

*He glared at her. "Damn it! You people don't take this seriously. I'm dead broke. We are nearly out of coal. And that damned Roosevelt has fixed it so I can't sell a load of wheat to buy coal!"*

*"Can we burn the wheat?" I asked.*

*I really wanted to know, but he glared at me again, so I said no more.*

*Cattle struggle to find something to eat in
this cornfield ruined by drought.*

Something had to be done for the economy. And Franklin Delano Roosevelt, who became president at the beginning of 1933, developed a plan to pull the country out of the Great Depression. His plan was called the New Deal. First, Roosevelt declared a bank holiday (closed down all the banks in the country) for a few days, allowing time to sort out the worst of the banking mess and to prevent more banks from failing. Then he started programs to help farmers as well as the unemployed, the poor, and the homeless—including some programs, such as Social Security, that still exist today. Still more programs were designed to heal the damage done to the land by years of careless farming, mining, and lumbering. The New Deal was more than the U.S. government had ever tried to do. Everything about it was new, and it was not always efficient. But the Great Depression was a big and terrible problem. The New Deal was accepted by an America that was ready for radical change.

**APRIL 25, 1934, WEDNESDAY:**
*Last weekend was the worst dust storm we ever had. We've been having quite a bit of blowing dirt every year since the drouth [drought] started, not only here, but all over the Great Plains. Many days this spring the air is just full of dirt coming, literally, for hundreds of miles. It sifts into everything. After we wash the dishes and put them away, so much dust sifts into the cupboards that we must wash them again before the next meal. Clothes in the closets are covered with dust.*

*Last weekend no one was taking an automobile out for fear of ruining the motor. I rode Roany to Frank's place to return a gear. To find my way I had to ride right beside the fence, scarcely able to see from one fence post to the next.*

*Newspapers say the deaths of many babies and old people are attributed to breathing in so much dirt.*

By the time President Roosevelt's New Deal programs began,
millions of Americans had been out of work for many months.
The first step in the economic recovery process was to help
the worker get back self-respect, as shown in this poster.

The town of Elkhart, Kansas, is engulfed by a dust storm in 1937. People who were out in such a storm had to keep their mouths and noses covered or else risk being smothered.

People could (and did) get lost in dust storms and smother to death. Far more people were victims of "dust pneumonia." Dust in the air would make a person with any sort of breathing problem or disease sicker. This would sometimes lead to pneumonia, which was often fatal.

**MAY 21, 1934, MONDAY:**
*Saturday, Dad, Bud, and I planted an acre of potatoes. There was so much dirt in the air I couldn't see Bud only a few feet in front of me. Even the air in the house was just a haze. In the evening the wind died down, and Cap came to take me to the movie. We joked about how hard it is to get cleaned up enough to go anywhere.*

**JULY 6, 1934, FRIDAY:**
*Bud . . . is very fed up and anxious to get away to school and fit himself for a job.*

*Poor Bud. He has worked so hard and saved so hard. He has done without nice clothes and never went to a dance or movie oftener than about once a year because he was saving every penny for college. He hoped his livestock would pay his way for four years. This year they are worth less, and he absolutely must sell them because there is not enough feed for them and no money to buy feed. All the stock he has won't pay his way through one year of college.*

Perhaps the saddest aspect of the Great Depression and the Dust Bowl was the broken dreams of the people who lived through it. Farmers and their families had moved to the Great Plains full of hope, pursuing the opportunity to own their own farms and to earn a comfortable and independent living from them. They wanted their children's lives to be easier, and they worked hard to make it all happen. Instead, they and their families worked harder and harder

*Laundry swinging in the breeze reveals that this farm in
Texas is still occupied, but many families abandoned
their farms rather than battle the dust storms and drought.*

[ 41 ]

and had less and less to show for it. Bud did better than most—he finally made it to college. But many on the Great Plains lost their farms and their dreams of independence completely.

JULY 18, 1934, WEDNESDAY:
*It is 104 degrees in the shade. The grain fields are all eaten up, so I'm herding the cows along the ditches of the roads. The garden is burned up. We don't dare carry water to it because the well is going dry and we need all the water there is for us and the livestock. The river is dry. We have fenced a lane from the Big Pasture to the lake so the beef cattle will have access to water.*

AUGUST 1, 1934, WEDNESDAY:
*Everything is just the same—hot and dry. . . .*

*The drouth and dust storms are something fierce. As far as one can see are brown pastures and fields which, in the wind, just rise up and fill the air with dirt. It tortures animals and humans, makes housekeeping an everlasting drudgery, and ruins machinery.*

*The crops are long since ruined. In the spring wheat section of the U.S., a crop of 12 million bushels is expected instead of the usual 170 million. . . . All subsoil moisture is gone. Fifteen feet down the ground is dry as dust. . . . Cattle and horses are dying, some from starvation and some from dirt they eat on the grass.*

*The government is buying cattle, paying $20.00 a head for cows and $4.00 for calves, and not buying enough to do much good.*

A New Deal program tried to prop up the cattle market by having the government itself buy some of the cattle the desperate farmers were trying to sell. This was just one of many New Deal efforts to cope with the farming crisis. Without these programs, many more farmers would have had to leave their farms. Still, farmers and others argued about whether the New Deal, taken altogether, did the farmers themselves much good. A lot of the government money directed at farmers ended up in the pockets of bankers and others who held mortgages on the farmers' property.

But one thing is certain: New Deal programs did a great deal of good for the land itself, undoing many of the agricultural mistakes that had helped to bring about the Dust Bowl.

# BIG PROBLEM,
# BIG SOLUTION

*T*HE DUST BOWL was a big problem, and it required a big solution. Hundreds of millions of tons of soil were blowing away from the Dust Bowl, never to return. New soil-saving techniques—especially those used to control wind erosion—needed to be used all over the Great Plains to make a difference. The problem sprawled across many states, and the federal government's New Deal tried to coordinate a nationwide solution.

Part of the solution was for the federal government to actually buy from farmers millions of acres of the most fragile land in the Dust Bowl—the land least suitable for growing wheat and other field crops. The idea was to stop plowing this land and instead allow permanent grasses to grow and hold the soil in place. Some of this land was allowed to return to its natural state and was added to the National Parks system. Some was turned into permanent pasture, with only a limited number of livestock permitted to graze on it.

The New Deal, through its Soil Conservation Service, also took steps to help heal the land the government didn't buy. Not only did the New Dealers give farmers good advice on soil conservation, but also many programs actually paid the farmers to take the advice and put conservation measures to work. Here are some of the techniques farmers used to help heal the damage of the Dust Bowl:

*Restoring pasture:* Farmers were encouraged to turn their most fragile and vulnerable land into permanent pasture or hayfields instead of plowing it. New Deal programs helped pay for reseeding the land with grasses. They also encouraged or required measures to keep the pastures in better condition, such as rotational grazing and limiting the number of animals per acre.

*No plowing until spring:* Crop residues—the plant stubble and debris left after harvest—were left on fields over the winter to hold the soil in place. This was a cheap and effective way to help prevent blowing.

*Rough tillage:* A rough surface resists blowing better than a smooth one, so farmers plowed their fields into furrows to prevent blowing and to help the soil to catch whatever rain might come. During the most windy time of year, this kind of tillage needs to be repeated every week to be effective. Many farmers couldn't afford the gas to run their tractors so often; a government program gave many of them the money to do this.

*Contour plowing:* This technique is very important for preventing wind and water erosion on any plowed field. On hilly land, furrows are plowed across the hill rather than up-and-down; this allows the furrows to slow down rainwater as it runs off down the hill. More water is absorbed by the soil, and less soil washes away. To prevent wind erosion on flat land, rough tillage furrows are plowed perpendicular to the direction that winds usually travel.

*Contour plowing of a soybean field.*

*Strip cropping:* Wide strips of contour-plowed field crops are alternated with strips of drought-resistant hay or sorghum. Rain runoff is slowed and absorbed by the grassy strips, and windblown dust is stopped by the grass before it can develop into drifts.

*Flood control:* It doesn't rain much on the Great Plains, but often when it does rain, it pours. Flooding can wash away crops and soil alike. The New Deal began building dams and funding other flood-control projects that not only controlled flooding but also caught and saved rainwater for later use. In the years since the Dust Bowl, these projects have provided irrigation water for crops, as well as drinking water and hydroelectric power for growing western cities.

*Tree planting:* The roots of trees hold soil in place, and lines of trees planted across the direction of prevailing winds help break the force of the wind and prevent soil erosion. Since the early days of the Homestead Act, the federal government had encouraged the planting of trees on the Great Plains, but these efforts were tiny compared to the millions of trees planted under such government programs as the Civilian Conservation Corps (CCC) in the 1930s.

New Deal farm programs did not always run smoothly and efficiently. They were designed in far-away Washington, D.C., and administered by thousands of bureaucrats—few of whom had ever been farmers. Mistakes were inevitable. Many people thought parts of the New Deal were foolish, wrongheaded, and even bad for the farmers.

Government programs designed to reduce farm production were especially controversial. New Dealers argued that too much wheat and beef and other farm goods flooding the market had caused prices to drop. Reduce the oversupply by growing and raising less

*An aerial view of strip cropping.*

*Through the efforts of the Civilian Conservation Corps, millions of trees were planted to help stop soil erosion throughout the Great Plains and the western states.*

farm produce, they said, and prices will rise, giving the farmer more money. Some people thought it was sinful to reduce the amount of food produced by American farmers while people all over the world went hungry. Sinful or not, these programs certainly hurt many farmers who rented their land. Government crop reduction money went only to landowners, not renters, and many tenant farmers were kicked off the land.

Still, from the point of view of the land itself, the New Deal's farm policies were a great success. Millions of farmers, desperate for improvement, adopted recommended soil conservation techniques. Most of these conservation methods were cheap and simple. Some had already been practiced by more prudent farmers for years.

And they made a difference. By 1937, soil conservation was widely practiced across the Great Plains. When good rains finally came in 1938, farmers planted soil-holding crops. By the spring of 1939, the Dust Bowl was smaller than it had been since 1932. Decent rainfall continued during 1939, and more rain than average fell all through the 1940s. Farmers continued to implement conservation measures, and the soil held. The Dust Bowl was over.

*A wind storm partially buried this 5-foot (1.5-meter) fence at a homestead in Kansas in 1954. Improved farming techniques have almost eliminated scenes like this.*

# The Dust Bowl of the 1950s

Droughts will come and go, and come again, but a Dust Bowl only happens when people mismanage the land in regions where little rain falls. The Dust Bowl of the 1930s should have made this a simple and obvious lesson—but not everybody learned and remembered it.

During the 1940s, rainfall was good across the Great Plains. World War II brought high prices and a great demand for grain and beef. Farmers responded by bringing in bumper crops—and by once again breaking millions of acres of sod on fragile, marginal land in order to grow these crops. A new Dust Bowl was just waiting to happen.

Then the rains stopped. By the winters of 1949 and 1950, the soil had dried out. The drought continued, and, in 1950, the first dust storms came.

It was a long drought, and dust storms continued until 1957, when the rains returned.

But Dust Bowl conditions in the 1950s never got as bad as they did during the 1930s. It turned out that farmers and the government had learned a great deal from the 1930s' Dust Bowl. They responded to the new Dust Bowl with the same kinds of conservation measures that had worked the last time—and this time they were able to identify the problems and respond much more quickly and with less trial and error.

The 1950s' Dust Bowl ended when the rains returned in 1957. But it is certain that drought will come again to this region. Only careful management of the land now and in the future can prevent a new Dust Bowl from happening when the next drought comes.

# 5

## CAN IT
## HAPPEN AGAIN?

$N$O DROUGHT on the Great Plains since the 1930s has been as severe as the drought that helped create the Dust Bowl. But periods of drought are part of the cycle of nature on the Great Plains, and sooner or later a terrible drought will come again.

Farmers now know how to farm in ways that conserve soil. So long as soil conservation techniques are practiced, the worst effects of the Dust Bowl need never happen again. In one newer technique, called no-till, seeds are planted without plowing. But although the events of the 1930s' Dust Bowl may never replay in exactly the same way, farmers must make sure that modern farming practices don't interact with nature to create new kinds of ecological catastrophes. Two such ecological problems of special concern to the Great Plains are groundwater contamination and groundwater depletion:

*Groundwater contamination:* Groundwater is water that lies under the soil. Sometimes groundwater is found only a few inches below the surface; in other places it's necessary to dig hundreds of feet before water is found. Groundwater is tapped by wells for irrigation and for drinking water for humans and animals. Most people who live outside of cities use groundwater for their drinking water.

Rainwater filters down through the soil to refill the groundwater aquifers. Contamination occurs when rainwater carries pollutants down into the groundwater. Once groundwater is polluted, it is very difficult to clean up.

A great deal of groundwater contamination comes from agricultural chemicals. Fertilizers and pesticides dissolve in rainwater and run off or soak into the ground. Theoretically, the soil slows down these dissolved chemicals, allowing them time to break down into harmless elements before they reach any underground aquifers. But scientists are now discovering that these chemicals travel down through the soil much faster than was believed years ago. And water samples now show that much of America's groundwater is already contaminated with fertilizer nitrates (nitrogen dissolved in water) or pesticides or both. In the Great Plains region, nitrate contamination is more common than pesticide contamination, and in some areas it is a very serious problem.

It has become clear that we must stop more fertilizers and pesticides from entering our water supply. Some states are beginning to step in with education and research programs (paid for by a tax on fertilizer sales) that help farmers with this. Nebraska has an especially tough anti-pollution law that restricts fertilizer use and requires farmers to test their water and soil. The U.S. Environmental Protection Agency (EPA) is slowly reviewing the effects on the environment of hundreds of pesticides; some pesticides have already been banned, and others will most likely be banned in the future.

*Groundwater depletion:* Groundwater depletion occurs when more water is taken out of an underground aquifer than is replaced by rainwater filtering down through the soil to refill the aquifer. In the long run, groundwater depletion will likely be an even greater threat to the Great Plains ecosystem than groundwater contamination— and it will also be a much more difficult problem to fix.

Most of the people now living where the Dust Bowl used to be get their drinking water from the Ogallala (or High Plains) aquifer. The Ogallala is the world's largest aquifer, stretching beneath thousands of square miles of South Dakota, Colorado, Kansas, Wyoming, Oklahoma, Nebraska, New Mexico, and Texas.

Two-hundred-thousand wells pump water out of the Ogallala aquifer. Some of this water goes to people's homes, but most of it is used to irrigate farmland and water livestock. Over much of the area that depends on the Ogallala for its water supply, more water is being pumped out of the wells than is being replaced by water trickling down through the soil to the aquifer. So far, the southern parts of the Ogallala aquifer have been hardest hit by this depletion. To find underground water in the Texas Panhandle, for example, you now have to drill a well 100 feet (30 meters) deeper than you did in 1930.

If we continue to take more water out of the Ogallala than nature replaces, sooner or later the water will run out. Without groundwater, modern farming—as well as towns and cities—would be impossible on the Great Plains.

What is being done to stop groundwater depletion? Although we have no national groundwater policy, some federal regulations do affect groundwater. State and local governments are largely responsible for setting the rules for groundwater use—but so far their efforts have not been enough to solve the depletion problem.

*Irrigation systems make it possible for dry areas to support
crops that once would have died from lack of water.*

The Great Plains' environmental problems are serious—but how serious? Some environmentalists believe that putting any cattle—or any conventional farms—at all on the more ecologically fragile parts of the Great Plains is a mistake that ought to be corrected. One radical idea, put forward by Rutgers University's Frank and Deborah Popper, is to give much of the prairie back to the bison. Their proposed Buffalo Commons nature preserve would be the world's largest national park (one and one-half times the size of California), covering parts of what used to be the Dust Bowl that are now in ecological and economic decline.

Many people—including most farmers—protest that such a radical solution to the region's current ecological problems isn't necessary. Farming, they say, can become more compatible with prairie ecology if farmers will use more and better conservation methods and consider planting new kinds of crops (especially perennial grains and mixed crops that mimic prairie vegetation) that are better suited to the Great Plains.

It is certain that drought will come again to the area that once was the Dust Bowl. And if the world is in fact getting warmer overall, as many scientists now believe, the problems associated with drought will tend to get worse. We will need to take great care to make sure that human activities don't team up with nature to create another ecological catastrophe in this region. The future will be shaped not only by nature, but also by us.

# Chronology

| | |
|---|---|
| Mid-1800s | Farmers from the eastern United States begin to settle on the Great Plains, plowing the prairie and planting wheat. |
| 1920 | Wheat prices drop. Farmers must plow and plant more just to break even. |
| 1929 | Stock market crashes, marking the beginning of the Great Depression. |
| 1931 | The record-breaking drought of the 1930s begins. |
| 1932 | Dust storms begin to occur. |
| January 1933 | Franklin Delano Roosevelt becomes president and starts many New Deal programs to cope with the Depression and the drought. |
| November 1933 | The first of the big dust storms covers many states in the Dust Bowl. |
| 1938 | Good rainfall returns and continues through the 1940s. The Dust Bowl shrinks and disappears. |

# Sources

Most of the research for this book was completed at Pittsburgh's excellent Carnegie Library and at the Library of Congress, in Washington. The most useful—and enjoyable—primary source I found was Ann Marie Low's *Dust Bowl Diary,* from which I have quoted extensively. Useful secondary sources included R. Douglas Hurt's *The Dust Bowl: An Agricultural and Social History* (Chicago, 1981) and Donald Worster's *Dust Bowl: The Southern Plains in the 1930s* (New York, 1979), as well as many books about other aspects of the 1930s—and about the earlier natural and human history of the region—that included bits of information relevant to the story of the Dust Bowl.

Much of my information about the ecology—and ongoing environmental problems—of the Dust Bowl region came from articles in journals oriented toward farming and environmental interests—journals as diverse as *Sierra* and *Successful Farming.* For the book's last chapter, especially, I relied heavily on journal articles, specifically those published in the USDA's *Farmline* (November 1991), *Successful Farming* (May 1988 and February 1990), *Nation's Business* (August 1983), and *Harrowsmith.*

# Further Reading

Glassman, Bruce. *The Crash of '29 and the New Deal*. Morristown, N.J.: Silver Burdett, 1986.

Katz, William Loren. *An Album of the Great Depression*. New York: Franklin Watts, 1978.

Lauber, Patricia. *Dust Bowl: The Story of Man on the Great Plains*. New York: Coward McCann, 1958.

Lawson, Don. *FDR's New Deal*. New York: Crowell, 1979.

Low, Ann Marie. *Dust Bowl Diary*. Lincoln: University of Nebraska Press, 1984.

Stein, R. Conrad. *The Story of the Great Depression*. Chicago: Childrens Press, 1985.

# Index